S0-DBC-415

WORLD SERIES CHAMPIONS

BALTIMORE ORIOLES

Published by Creative Education
P.O. Box 227, Mankato, Minnesota 56002
Creative Education is an imprint of The Creative Company
www.thecreativecompany.us

Design and production by Blue Design
Printed in the United States of America

Photographs by Corbis (Bettmann), Getty Images (Jonathan Daniel, Louis DeLuca/MLB Photos,
Diamond Images, Jerry Driendl, Focus on Sport, Bob Gomel//Time Life Pictures, Brad Mangin/
MLB Photos, TED MATHIAS/AFP, Ronald C. Modra/Sports Imagery, Doug Pensinger/Allsport,
Hy Peskin/Time Life Pictures, Photofile/MLB Photos, Rich Pilling/MLB Photos, Herb Scharfman/
Sports Imagery, Ezra Shaw, Jamie Squire, Perry Thorsvik, Tony Tomsic/MLB Photos, Hank
Walker//Time Life Pictures, Nick Wass)

Library of Congress Cataloging-in-Publication Data

Frisch, Aaron.
Baltimore Orioles / by Aaron Frisch.
p. cm. — (World Series champions)
Includes index.
ISBN 978-1-58341-692-1
1. Baltimore Orioles (Baseball team)—History—Juvenile literature. I. Title. II. Series.

GV875.B2F75 2009
796.357'64097526—dc22   2008003764

First edition
9 8 7 6 5 4 3 2 1

Cover: Outfielder Nick Markakis (top), third baseman Brooks Robinson (bottom)
Page 1: Second baseman Brian Roberts
Page 3: Shortstop Miguel Tejada

WORLD SERIES CHAMPIONS

BALTIMORE ORIOLES

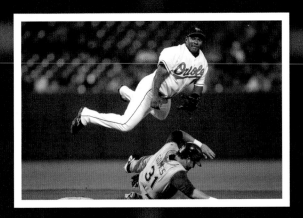

AARON FRISCH

CREATIVE EDUCATION

The Orioles are a team in **Major League Baseball**. They play in Baltimore, Maryland. Baltimore is a city on the East Coast. It is almost 300 years old.

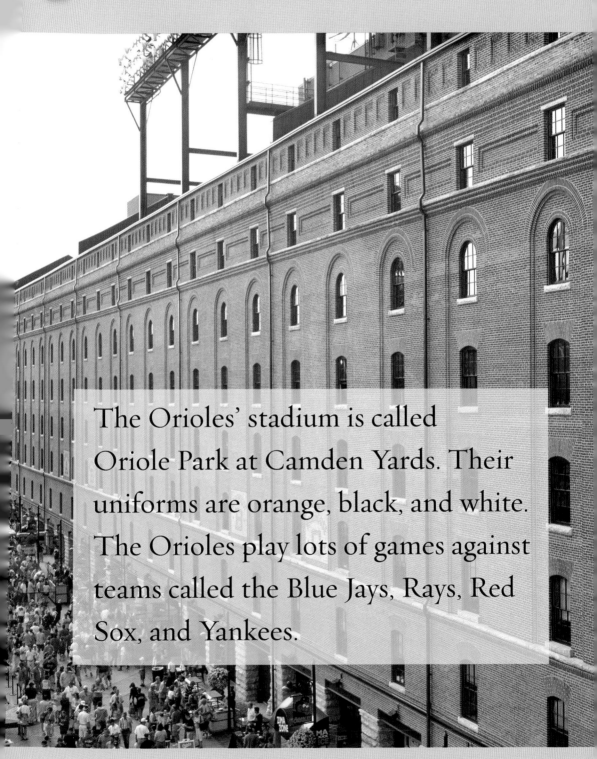

The Orioles' stadium is called Oriole Park at Camden Yards. Their uniforms are orange, black, and white. The Orioles play lots of games against teams called the Blue Jays, Rays, Red Sox, and Yankees.

GEORGE SISLER

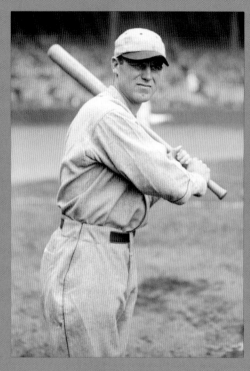

The Orioles started out in 1902 as a team called the Browns. The Browns played in St. Louis, Missouri. First baseman George Sisler (*SIZ-ler*) got lots of hits for the Browns. But they lost a lot of games.

FIRST BASEMAN
BOOG POWELL

9

SHORTSTOP
RON HANSEN

The Browns finally got to the World Series in 1944. But they lost. Ten years later, the Browns moved to Baltimore. They were renamed the Orioles.

THIRD BASEMAN
BROOKS ROBINSON

The Orioles got better in Baltimore. They added a third baseman named Brooks Robinson. He was great at diving to grab the ball.

Pitcher Jim Palmer

Outfielder Frank Robinson and pitcher Jim Palmer helped the Orioles get to the World Series in 1966 and 1969. They won the World Series in 1966 but lost in 1969. Then, in 1970, they won the World Series again!

OUTFIELDER
FRANK ROBINSON

15

EDDIE MURRAY

Eddie Murray was a good first baseman in the 1970s. He hit lots of home runs. Cal Ripken Jr. joined the Orioles in 1982. He was a shortstop who played good defense. He played in 2,632 straight games without missing any! That is a baseball **record**.

WORLD SERIES CHAMPIONS

BALTIMORE ORIOLES

CAL RIPKEN JR.

17

SECOND BASEMAN
BRIAN ROBERTS

The Orioles won the World Series again in 1983. They beat a team called the Phillies. Then the Orioles got worse. In 1988, they lost their first 21 games. But outfielder Brady Anderson helped them play better again. The Orioles got to the **playoffs** in 1996 and 1997.

OUTFIELDER
BRADY ANDERSON

21

PITCHER
JEREMY GUTHRIE

Pitcher Jeremy Guthrie was
another good Orioles player.
Outfielder Nick Markakis was
a star, too. He was a **slugger**
who played in the outfield.
Baltimore fans hope that
today's Orioles will win the
World Series again soon!

GLOSSARY

Major League Baseball — a group of 30 baseball teams that play against each other; major-league teams have the best players in the world

playoffs — games that are played after the season to see which team is the champion

record — something that is the best or most ever

slugger — a baseball player who is strong and can hit the ball hard

ORIOLES FACTS

Team colors: orange, black, and white

First home stadium (in Baltimore): Memorial Stadium

Home stadium today: Oriole Park at Camden Yards

League/Division: American League, Eastern Division

First season in Baltimore: 1954

World Series championships: 1966, 1970, 1983

Team name: The Orioles got their name because they play in Maryland. Orioles are birds with bright orange feathers. There are lots of orioles in Maryland. They are the state bird.

Major League Baseball Web site for kids:
http://www.mlb.com/mlb/kids/

INDEX